Dakota Dreams

written and illustrated by JANET HOWE TOWNSLEY

South Dakota State Historical Society Press   PIERRE

Dakota Dreams

Fannie Sabra Howe's Own Story

1881-1884

Partial funding for *Dakota Dreams* was provided by the
Mary Chilton Chapter, National Society Daughters of the
American Revolution, through the Mary Chilton DAR
Foundation, Sioux Falls, S.Dak.

Library of Congress Cataloging-in-Publication Data
is available on request.

Printed in the United States of America

03 04 05 06 07 08 09 10 11   9 8 7 6 5 4 3 2 1

With gratitude and appreciation for those

who came before: C. M., F. A., and Charles.

This account is for those who follow:

my children—Stuart, Barbara, Roy, Susan—

and my grandchildren—Gavin, Mikel, Jovanna,

Charles, Hannah, and Andrew.

Contents

1

Going to Dakota

The steam engine puffed and chugged and slowly pulled the train from the station. Fannie pressed her nose against the window and waved to her cousins on the platform until they disappeared in a cloud of white steam. Then she sat back in her seat and smiled. At last she was on her way to Dakota! School was finally over, and she was going to join her parents and brother Frank who had gone on ahead to claim their homestead.

1883 MAP OF RAILROADS TO SPINK COUNTY

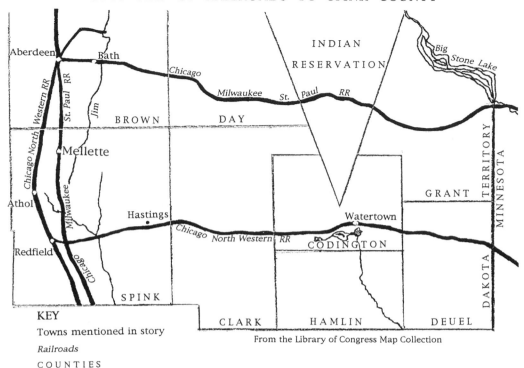

KEY
Towns mentioned in story
Railroads
COUNTIES

From the Library of Congress Map Collection

It was 1881. Railroads were being built, and families were moving west into the Dakota Territory to stake their claim for new farmland under the Homestead Act. Land for free! One hundred and sixty acres—a quarter of a square mile of flat, rich soil for those who came to claim their quarter and stayed to improve the land. It was a great opportunity.

Fannie's father had received an encouraging letter from his friend, Hall Spink, who had gone to Dakota Territory from Mazomanie, Wisconsin, three years earlier. "No stones, no trees—the land is good," Mr. Spink wrote. "Where there are wells, the water is good. There is a good chance to make money here if you have some capitol to begin with." He sent township maps that marked where the railroads were entering Dakota and building the new town of Mellette. "I expect there to be a great rush to claim lands," he said. Pa, Ma, and Frank had left as quickly as possible to beat the rush.

The open prairie land called not only to eastern farmers but also to skilled craftsmen and tradesmen, young and old, looking for a fresh start with new flat land. Even people from foreign countries could claim a quarter section from the United States government if they signed papers to become American citizens. Fannie had read the railroad advertisements in the Wisconsin newspapers, and every town back east had been flooded with posters that shouted the news:

LAND FOR FREE
OUR NEW RAILROAD CAN TAKE YOU THERE
FOR JUST PENNIES A MILE!

Fannie looked around at the other passengers on the train. There were two Swedish families, and a German family with six children. Mr. Spink's letter had said that the settlers near Mellette were mostly Americans, but there were also two Norwegians, and a German settlement had started up nearby. From her new carpet bag, Fannie pulled out a small book and began to write on its blank pages:

August 1, 1881
Going to Dakota! . . . An English family from Canada on the train [is also] bound for Watertown. . . . Cars crowded all the way.

Fannie's father, Charles Morgan Howe, saw great promise in the new Dakota Territory, and he was not afraid of hard work. His children had often heard the stories of how, as a

Congress passed the Homestead Act in 1862 to give public lands to small farmers. Any head of a family, or a single man or woman over twenty-one, could claim a quarter section of vacant government land for a two-dollar filing fee. The government required that the settler live on the land, build some kind of house (at least eight feet by ten feet in size), dig a well, break the soil, and grow crops. After five years, the homesteader would own the land. Another law allowed homesteaders to buy a quarter section of land for one dollar and twenty-five cents an acre after working it for only six months. This was called a preemption claim. Homesteaders could then claim another quarter section, increasing their landholding. These laws allowed thousands of people to move onto western lands that had once been the home of American Indians. By 1881, wars and treaties with the United States government had pushed most of the tribes out of eastern Dakota Territory.

very young man, he had left his native Vermont and gone to sea on a whaling ship to earn enough money so he could marry his sweetheart, Mary Jane Bickford. During frequent moves over the years, Fannie's parents had started several small stores. They now owned a successful lumberyard in Wisconsin. Like many other businessmen, Fannie's father knew that the Dakota homesteaders would need farming equipment, seed for their crops, and lumber for their new homes. Their wives would want needles and thread, calico for their clothes and curtains, and pots and pans for their kitchens. The new town of Mellette would need stores.

Soon trains would be able to haul supplies from the East Coast to Mellette and return to the eastern markets with grain and produce from the new farms. The prairie was the land of the future, and now Fannie was going to see it, too! The long train ride from Mazomanie, Wisconsin, to Watertown on the edge of the Dakota Territory would take two days and one night. Because the promised new train route to Mellette was not yet finished, Pa would meet Fannie in Watertown. The last of her journey to their homestead near Mellette would be by horse and wagon and would take two more days.

There was no dining car on the train. Instead it stopped three times a day for twenty minutes for passengers to get off and buy a meal. A track-side cafe would be ready with a set meal, for there was no time to make choices. People had to eat whatever was served quickly, pay their bill, and hurry back onto the train to continue their journey.

Like many of the other people on the train, Fannie brought along food to eat. Her bundle had been carefully packed, stuffed with hunks of dried apples and chicken, crusts of bread, and a jam-layered spice cake her aunt had made. The ginger cookies had gotten quite crushed, but Fannie devoured every delicious crumb.

When the train stopped for the evening meal, Fannie got off to stretch her legs. She hoped that would help her sleep, but, alas, the man behind her snored loudly all night long.

The next morning she wrote in her diary:

August 2
I didn't sleep much last night.

Fannie knew that Dakota would be different from her home in the Wisconsin woods or her grandparent's home amid the green hills of Vermont. She pondered but could not yet picture what the prairie would be like. After the breakfast stop, she watched the land glide by her window and noted the changes.

Can not say I admire this flat treeless country. It was rocky until we reached Minnesota.

Now the hills flattened out, the many trees became few, and the stops between towns became farther apart. It all seemed so strange. The noonday meal was in Marshall, Minnesota, and the last stop would be Watertown. Fannie silently cheered, *hooray.*

2

Friendly Strangers and Bedbugs

Papa was waiting at the Watertown station. "Fannie!" he boomed as she stepped from the train and he enveloped her in a bear hug. He introduced her to the smiling men standing by. "You remember Mr. Spink from Mazomanie, and this is our new neighbor here, Mr. Treadway." Pa loaded Fannie's trunk into his wagon, which was already filled with needed supplies for their homesteads. "Now let's all go get some supper."

Pa explained that Mr. Treadway had worked on his own land claim, and now, like many other settlers, he was anxious to hire out to another homesteader to earn some desperately needed cash. "He has been a great help to me," said Pa.

Later that night before Fannie turned off her lamp, she wrote in her dairy:

Arrived at last! . . . After supper we went for a walk. . . .
How strange it seemed without any trees.

She paused and thought about all the different things she had seen. The busy new town of Watertown seemed raw and only half-finished. The muddy roads had deep ruts carved out from the constant pressure of overloaded wagon wheels. Buildings were in various stages of construction amid piles of tin cans and packing boxes. The town center had long rows of drab, square-fronted stores, offices, and restaurants. Their wooden fronts were already streaked from the smoke of soft coal. Tar paper covered their sides. At the edge of town, a village of tents and covered wagons had sprung up. Fannie wondered if the new town of Mellette would look like this.

She was not overjoyed with her hotel room, and her bed sheets looked dirty.

Our rooms do not compare favorably with such a fashionable
place as the Carlisle House, but I guess we shall live through

it. . . . Took off the undersheet and used the upper one for the
under and the white spread for a top sheet.

Early the next morning, they all climbed into the wagon for the last seventy-five miles of the journey. The team of horses pulling the heavy wagon could only cover about thirty-seven miles a day. Pa had called this prairie flat as a pancake and the way straight as an arrow. Here and there were a few trees, but the unbroken sky seemed immense over the endless prairie grasses. Fannie breathed in deeply the fresh, sweet smell of this virgin land.

There were no highways to follow—only the wagon tracks of earlier travelers. No fences marked the boundaries of the few huts they passed, and there were no motels or hotels. One had to rely on a few friends, as well as strangers, who opened their small houses to travelers for simple meals or to spend the night. All this was new to Fannie.

August 3
Had a good sleep even if things were
dirty. . . . We started at 15 minutes to
8. . . . and Lo and behold, a few miles
out Hall Spink picked 15 bed bugs off
his coat. [Pa] found 2, and I found a
mammoth one on my ulster. . . .

Rode only about 20 miles to Widow
Thompson's, and Mr. Treadway was
so sick we had to stay over three hours.
My head ached hard, too, but I lay
down and had cold water on my head
and felt very well the rest of the day.

9

GOOD NIGHT, SLEEP TIGHT
DON'T LET THE BEDBUGS BITE

This silly rhyme was no joke to early travelers. A cloth bag stuffed with hay, corn husks, or prairie grass and placed on a hard wooden plank often served as a mattress. Such beds made perfect hiding places for these small wingless, blood-sucking insects. Bedbugs were only about one-fifth of an inch long and could hide in cracks or mattress seams during the day. At night they crawled out to feed upon a warm sleeping body. The next day the person was covered with itchy welts. The swellings were due to an allergic reaction to fluids injected by the bug while feeding. The bite of a bedbug was not thought to cause any diseases, but it was no laughing matter to a person covered with bites.

Mrs. Thompson's house is a little wooden house of 3 rooms—a kitchen, diningroom, and bedroom. A portion of the kitchen serves as a bedroom and is separated from the other bedroom by some boards with a bed quilt spread over them. . . . The house isn't plastered, neither has it a carpet. In the bedroom is a little melodeon upon which I played a tune before I had my [noonday] dinner. . . . My heart was made glad by the old familiar melody, "Oh Dem Golden Slippers."

We went on 16 miles further . . . and stopped at Mike Kelly's. . . . The house was much in the condition of Mrs. Thompson's— small. Mrs. Kelly was very kind to us. She put clean sheets on our beds. Something you don't see done very often for strangers.

August 4

We started out [this] morning at a quarter to 5. . . . We arrived at Hastings, 20 miles farther on, at 8 o'clock. The house we stopped at was the nicest of any we have stopped at yet. There was a rag carpet on the floor [and] white curtains looped back with red strips with white beads. The cutest part of it was Mrs. Lang's bedroom. It was a little corner of the sitting room and two white curtains with a strip of red on the edge obscured the bed from view. They have just started a little grocery store and are going to make it larger soon. . . . Everyone seems so cordial here—so different from Mazo.

After we were about 5 miles from Hastings, we got mired in Dry Run.

Dry run was full of mud. After much pushing and shoving, they got the wagon off without serious damage. The swollen

James River and its uneven current almost caused another problem.

As we were crossing the Jim River on the ferry, I nearly fell over backwards into the water. Got to Hall Spink's about 4 o'clock . . . and stayed all night as it looked like rain. That was my first night in a dug out.

And what a different kind of house it was. Hall had dug a hole in the side of the bank near the river for his house. The front wall was made of bricks of sod, which he had cut and placed with the matted grass on the outside. It was very dark inside with just one small window. Fannie thought that it was surprisingly cool in spite of the hot sun outside. "We are going

to plaster the walls with sand and lime, which will make it lighter inside," Hall explained. The floor was dirt that had been pounded hard but still needed to be swept often with a willow broom to keep the dust down. Fannie looked up and noticed a square of canvas placed under the sod roof above the small table. Mrs. Spink laughed, "That's to keep bits of dirt from falling into my soup."

HASTINGS

Like many early towns, Hastings can no longer be found on a modern map. Although the town was first started in 1879, the Chicago & North Western Railroad did not run its track through the town. Instead the railroad built its road a mile south. The businesses in early towns could not survive without a railroad. The fate of Hastings was further sealed when fire destroyed all the town's buildings in 1884. People like Mrs. Lang did not rebuild. They moved to Mellette or Redfield to be next to the railroad.

3

Our Prairie Home

It was good to see Ma and Frank again. Pete, the dog, ran circles around Pa in his joy at having him back. And there was a surprise—they had no house or dugout on their land, but a tent instead! The horses, Flora, Jack, Ranger, and Star, were tethered a short distance away near the farm equipment. Frank was as anxious to show Fannie around their homestead as she was to see it. Pa placed Fannie's trunk next to her cot in the tent while Frank got the horses ready.

As they rode, Frank talked excitedly about the quarters of land he and Pa had selected. He pointed out the stakes they had driven in the ground at each corner, and the horses followed the wide furrows plowed around the outer edges that marked their claims. Frank and Pa had registered their claims

at the Government Land Office in Watertown. "Not much of a town yet, is it," he asked, "but you just wait, 'cause the area is growing fast, and it's the best place in the Dakota Territory!"

Frank made it all sound quite simple and fun, but Fannie knew how hard they had worked, and the hardest part was yet to come. They had to make all the improvements required by the Homestead Act before the land could become theirs. "First we will put in a well," Frank said. "We're working on that now, and then we start breaking the sod. In the fall, after we get the last hay harvested for the animals, Pa'll start building a timber house and barn—not just a shanty, but a real house."

"Oh, Papa, there is a lot for us to do!" Fannie exclaimed when they got back to the tent. "Yes, and it will be your job to help Ma prepare the meals for our little band," he answered. Ma laughed, "We cook and eat outside and hope it doesn't rain."

August 5
Mosquitoes were awful. . . . I took a walk . . . about one-half
mile. Got some wild flowers.

Fannie was enchanted by the patches of yellow black-eyed
susans, white beard tongues, and daisies clustered amid the
clover and buffalo grass. She picked a bouquet of prairie
phlox, purple cornflowers, and goldenrod. Ma had told her
that in the spring the prairie had been a carpet of colorful
wildflowers with pink and violet pasque flowers, mariposa lil-
ies, violets, and thickets of wild plums. "Clumps of wild roses
and chokecherry shrubs grow down near the river, too," Ma
said.

August 6
Pa and Frank were both sick with dysentery and haven't got
well yet. If it hadn't been for that, I should have been perfectly
content here in our tent. We have no well, so Mr. Treadway has
to go over to the railroad well for water. We had millions of
mosquitoes to see us last night. My hands and face are covered
with bites. . . . Mr. T. is trying to dig a well. [It's] down about
5 ft. now. Looks rather dubious about getting water.

chokecherry

purple
coneflower

wild
plum

violet

pasque   goldenrod   mariposa lilly   clover   wild geranium   beardtongue   blackeyed susan

17

People treated dysentery and other stomach problems in many different ways. Some bought medicines or tonics from drug companies, but most people made their own from local plants and herbs. In Vermont, Fannie had gathered blackberry roots in the fall for her grandmother. These were made into a tea. They were simmered in a pint of water until the water turned dark. Another tonic common in New England was made from boiled seeds of the barberry (or berberry) bush. On the prairie, homesteaders learned about local remedies. Some American Indians boiled sumac berries as a potion for sore throats, coughs, burns, and diarrhea. Blackfeet Indians made a tea from the sagebrush. Some European settlers brewed fetid marigold leaves for upset stomachs, as they had in the old country. In the 1880s, there was no proven cure. People often had to let nature take its course.

The bottle of Ayers Sarsaparilla was empty, so Ma brewed some strong mint tea instead, using the dried mint leaves she had brought from Wisconsin. She handed Frank and Pa a cup of her hot tonic and hoped they would feel better soon. Fannie made another note in her diary.

Pa and Frank are a little better, I think. Allie and Eliza Newell came over this afternoon and stayed a long time. Seemed funny to be so far away from home on Sunday. No church or anything within a good many miles.

The Newells were friends from Mazomanie who had come out to homestead with their mother, Jane, and brother, Arthur. Pa was glad to see them. "Ask that big brother of yours to come on over if he has the time," Pa said, "to give me a hand with this well. Be much obliged."

4

Problems! All is Not Well

August 8
Went over to see Allie. Had a nice ride and enjoyed my visit. Pa &
Frank are better today. It is very warm.

August 9
Arthur Newell came over this morning to help Treadway dig the
well. Oh, for some water! Prairie, Prairie, all around and not a
drop of water to drink. Mosquitoes are awful. I am all bit up
from north to south.

August 10
Arthur is here again and still no water. He and Treadway went
after a well auger. They found water after boring 18 feet. [The
well] commenced to cave in. They had to give it up.

August 11
Treadway is gone to Bath for lumber [to shore up the sides of
the well]. Frank is reading. The wind blows nice this morning.

August 12
Mosquitoes were awful last night. We couldn't get any sleep.
They sang so loud and bit so hard. Mr. Treadway hasn't got
back. Pete mourns for him. He has been lying out by the well
all of the afternoon.

August 13
[Treadway] got back after nine o'clock last night. We were just gone to sleep & of course did not feel pleasant to be routed out. Ma had to get up and get [him] some supper.

Water was desperately needed for the animals. Pa and Frank filled the wagon with empty barrels and drove four miles to the Jim River. They were disappointed that the water was murky and warm.

Oh, for a nice cool drink of pure water!

August 14
We moved [our tent] one-half mile nearer the [railroad] track. Treadway mowed all around and it looks like a pretty lawn. It is so much nicer than where we were before. . . . Was going to write [a letter] but had to stop and get lunch for the folks.

5

What's for Breakfast (Lunch, or Supper)?

On August 13, Fannie had confided to her diary,

I do not feel good, for like a fool I ate too much canned mackerel for breakfast.

The family's usual Wisconsin breakfast of mush with milk was now a rare treat, and brown sugar was an even rarer luxury. What little milk there was came from a neighbor's cow.

Because they had no well, they collected rain water in wooden barrels for drinking. A gunny sack was placed over the mouth of each barrel and held tight by a steel hoop. This protected the drinking water from dirt. Fannie thought the hot rays of a relentless sun made the water taste bad. She hoped that lemon juice would mask the taste. She asked Pa and Frank to buy some lemons on their trip to see the new town of Mellette.

I got four little lemons for 40 cents, very little too. [I] sent for 6 lemons but I guess we exhausted the town as it was. . . . The new town consists of part of a [railroad] switch—big city!!

August 14
We had a light lunch and Pa, Ma, and I went over to Hall's and got some potatoes, cucumbers, corn and ripe tomatoes.

The family had not had potatoes for over a week. Since Ma had not been able to plant a garden in time to grow summer vegetables, they had to purchase them from the neighbors' garden. Fannie often went with Ma to the Spinks to buy their melons and whatever other fresh vegetables they had—beets, turnips, and carrots. Pumpkins would be ready in the early fall.

Farm families always tried to preserve their summer fruits and vegetables for the long winter months. Root vegetables

---

CANNED FOODS

Canning as a way of preserving food began in 1809 in France. It soon spread to other countries, and in 1822, William Underwood of Boston started packing fruits and vegetables in hand-blown glass bottles. Twenty years later, tin cans were first used. By the 1880s, canned fruits, meat, fish, and milk were readily available in stores. To preserve food in this way, it had to be heated to kill germs. Then it was packed in airtight glass jars or tin cans. The food could then be eaten whenever fresh food was not available. Canned foods were part of the staples that settlers like the Howe's brought to Dakota Territory.

could be stored in a cool dark place. As a young child in Wisconsin, Fannie had often helped dry apples by hanging slices dipped in lemon juice on a string. Some meats could be preserved when dried, smoked, or soaked in salt. Because there was no way to keep fresh meat from spoiling in the heat, some of the family's food came from tin cans. Underwood Deviled Ham was a favorite. Fannie's parents had brought supplies of flour and sugar, coffee beans, salt, and food in tins with them.

Because of the very real danger of fire, Ma and Pa had set up their cooking area outside. Much of their food was boiled in

iron pots over an open fire in a cleared area. Large kettles were hung on a hook from a pole supported at each end by a forked stick. Fire wood was hard to come by on the prairie, so they used what ever they could find. Fannie collected buffalo chips as she took her walks on the prairie. Twigs, sunflower stalks, and dried corn cobs were also used as fuel.

Ma showed Fannie how to bake outside with a "spider," or Dutch oven. The deep, large kettle had three legs and a tight, flat lid. "It's not so different from cooking inside a house," Ma said. "You place the pot down on the ground over glowing coals. Then you cover the lid with more coals so that the heat comes from both the top and bottom."

Fannie watched her mother making pies:

She showed me how to make the crust flaky. I guess I had better put it down lest I forget it. After she rolls the crust out, she spreads lard on it and sprinkles flour over that, pressing it down with her fingers.

Salt, flour, cornmeal, sugar, and coffee beans were stored in brown crocks or jars with tight lids. Wooden pails and buckets held apples and root vegetables. Heavy iron skillets were used for frying over the open fire. Fannie saw the tinware bread pans and knew in time she would be making bread almost daily, just as she had done in Wisconsin.

Dishes and mugs for coffee, and various size bowls were kept on shelves that Frank had made out of their wooden packing boxes. Ma had tacked bright calico material over the open shelves to help keep out the prairie dust. Pa and Frank had tied a canvas lean-to next to their tent to give some protection from the weather for the cooks and their supplies.

On the shelf were cake pans with an open center tube that prevented the cake from having an uncooked center. Fannie knew that preparing foods would be easier with the metal grater, colander, and strainer Ma had brought along on their homesteading adventure. She had also packed a wooden whisk for whipping eggs, a potato masher, and spoons, ladles, and scoops of different sizes.

Molasses came in wooden barrels and was ladled into a small pitcher for daily use. It was tasty on mush or corn bread. When they had no butter, they mixed lard with molasses for a

In 1881, you could only buy whole coffee beans. You had to grind them yourself with a hand grinder. The Howe family used a coffee grinder that looked like this.

spread. Apple butter—sliced sugared apples boiled until thick—was a favorite treat and had been easy to make in Wisconsin. On the prairie, chokecherry jam, made from berries growing along the creeks, was a substitute.

Pa and Frank set traps for small animals such as prairie chickens and jack rabbits for meat. They trapped beavers, otters, and muskrats, as well as coyotes, wolves, and foxes, for skins. Pa said there were wild ducks and geese in the spring and fall. Most buffalo had been killed, but there were still deer and antelope around. Pa and Frank were not hunters, but other homesteaders were.

William Waterbury, who had a homestead claim two miles north of Pa's, became a good friend over a hearty meal. Waterbury and his brother Eugene would go duck hunting with Treadway. The brothers' homestead was not as well equipped

as Pa's, and they did not have a mowing machine. Treadway suggested that they ask to borrow Pa's. Busy with his own mowing, Pa said no when they asked to use the mower.

The next Sunday, Waterbury told Treadway to bring Pa up to their claim for supper. The brothers brought in a good supply of ducks and started to dress and cook them. Pa and William sat down first. "The way we ate," Waterbury told Fannie, "I guess the cooks thought there wouldn't be any ducks left for them." When the meal ended, Pa turned on his bench and said, "Anything I have down at my place that you want, come down and get it!"

The two men were friends after that, and Ma often had wild ducks cooking in the spider.

6

Too Hot, Too Cold, Too Wet, Too Windy

August 15

Pa and Treadway started off about 7 o'clock for Bath to get the rest of their traps. Pete ran after them and Treadway had to come back with him. We had him chained, but I gave him his breakfast and thought they were far enough away so he wouldn't follow and unchained him. He is here now, contented to stay. . . .

It seems a little lonesome without Pa. Ma is combing my hair while I write and I feel refreshed by it.

Fannie usually crimped her hair in tight curls and waves in the latest style. Here on the prairie she did not bother with the crimping pins. It was just easier to let her hair hang loose in the wind or pull it back with a ribbon.

August 16
It rained again last night. Was raining when I went to sleep. . . .
We were a lazy crew this morning. It was too hot to work. My
face is as rough as a nutmeg grater. Who needs one? I am at
your service. Frank made points on the two broken blades of my
knife this morning. I turned the grindstone.

It was fiercely hot. The blazing August sun beat down by day, and the nights turned suddenly cold when the prairie winds brought rain. Fannie slept with Ma's quilt over her and the buffalo coat at the foot of her bed. She liked to read the names written on the blocks of the remembrance quilt that her Vermont family and friends had given her mother so long ago.

August 17
Pa got home about 6:30 p.m. He hadn't been here but about 5
minutes when it commenced to rain real hard and it kept it up,
too, for several hours. Rained again all this morning and was
very cold and damp in the tent. There was a leaky spot over
Frank's bed which let in considerable water.

Needless to say, Frank was not pleased. A somber sky, wet bedding, and rain all morning long deadened their spirits. Later when the sun showed its face, Pa plowed the first furrow on the land. The family all went down by their old camping place to watch him plow.

HERE IS A QUILT
TO REMEMBER US BY

When Mary Jane Bickford married Charles Morgan
Howe in 1856, the couple moved far away to Wisconsin.
Family and friends gave the new bride a remembrance
quilt. Such gifts were also called friendship or album
quilts. Each square was stitched by hand and signed by
its maker. Many quilters added a small verse or a parting
thought in ink. Some of the squares on Ma's quilt had
such sayings. Here are two examples:

> Mary, we soon will be parted
> And friendship ties of youth be rent.
> Our farewell flow of tears be started
> When you be westward sent.
>
> A dear friend soon will leave
> We will sadly miss her here.

33

7

Time to Hay, a Time for Play

August 18

A lovely morning and we improved it by taking a ride, all of us, to look after a good haying spot. It was a lovely ride and I enjoyed so much the air, made me feel so refreshed. On our way home we found a place where someone had [camped], and Pa set fire to it [to clean it up] and left it to its own destruction. The result was he had to fight fire till he nearly melted.

A sudden gust of wind had fanned Pa's small fire, and it was lucky the ground was still a bit damp from the rain shower of yesterday. Dry grass would have been much harder to put out.

Frank is driving the reaper this afternoon and Treadway the rake. [Ma & Pa and I went out and raked hay.] Poor Jack is left alone and is making a great fuss. Poor-old-broken-hearted horse knows not why he was left alone. . . . I am being eaten alive by the mosquitoes, but the winds of the north help, and we are all happy to be in the fields on this beautiful prairie.

August 19
We saw a train on the St. Paul track last night. It came by here and then went back to the site of the new town and left three cars filled with lumber [to build the railroad station]. This morning Ma, Pa and I went over to the well near there for water. There were two men unloading lumber. One said the [rail]road would bring lumber for anyone on this road, for which we are very glad.

The most welcome news— the well was finally finished and working. This time the sides were lined with wooden casings to shore it up. The men built these in twelve-foot sections on the ground. They put the wood together with the same circumference as the well hole they had dug. The wooden sections were put down, one at a time, into the well. A two-by-four was

nailed across the top of the well, and Frank attached a metal
pulley to it and tied a bucket to the end of the rope. At last! The
family had their own water—cool, wet, wonderful water.

*Ma & I went out and settled the haystack this morning. Ma
is now driving the [horse rake] and thinks it lots of fun. The
three men are unloading and stacking hay.... Today we have a
south wind which helps us. It is quite cool where I am out of the
sun.... The skies appear partially covered with black clouds. It
rains off and on but the sun returns to say to us, "I have not disappeared forever."*

August 20

We discovered yesterday that the water in our well was better than any around here. It is very cool. I tell you it seems good to have a good cool drink once more.

We have a new neighbor—just came today—a young man from New York. His land joins Treadway's. He came with a yoke of oxen and squatted. Expects more things soon. He just went by whistling. . . .

Pa and Treadway got in 5 loads of hay yesterday and 5 today. They will get in one more, perhaps two more, before dark, and then they will have 10 tons, perhaps more.

August 21

We all four went out for a ride this morning to see the tree claims around us, to see if their owners had done the required amount of work on them.

A homesteader could claim an extra one hundred sixty acres of land under the Timber Culture Act. He or she had to pay fourteen dollars, plant forty acres of trees, and keep them growing for eight years. This was called a tree claim. It proved so difficult to keep trees alive on the dry prairie that the law was changed from forty to ten acres. Willow, cottonwood, and wild plum trees were planted most often in Dakota.

How they laughed when they saw the poor saplings. Withered and bent, they looked like bare sticks rather than young trees. They all agreed that the trick would be to keep the trees alive and growing for eight years in this arid land.

For supper we had some potatoes cooked with pork. It was late [and dark] when we left the table and the dishes weren't washed very well. The poor dog, Peter, has his front paws scratched or sore from the prairie grass. He is a very agreeable dog and never bites except when playing.

August 23
Ma and I rode down in the hay rack with Pa and Treadway, then Ma went to raking while Pa and Frank loaded the wagon. I sat in front and let them pile the hay all up around me. When the wagon was loaded, we all got up on top of the load and road up to the haystack. . . . There we were, a good ways to the ground

with no ladder nor anything to help us down with. For awhile it looked rather dubious about getting down, but Treadway drove the wagon close up to the haystack. Then we slid down into the wagon without any trouble.

Laughing and chuckling, they discovered that prairie hay was sharp and scratchy. But it would make good food for the animals next winter.

8

The Unexpected
An Axle Breaks and a Fire

A strong prairie wind had started early in the day on August twenty-second. It whipped Fannie's skirt and hair and pushed her about as she worked in the hay field. Clouds of dust rose from plowed fields hiding the low sun of early morning. Wind speeds of twenty to thirty miles an hour were not unusual here on the prairie, but on this day they brought trouble.

> *It is fearful windy today, the windiest day we have seen in Dakota. They are trying to plow today as the wind prevents haying, but the plow doesn't work very well.*

> *I have been sitting out in the shade of the haystack—came in to drive Flora away from the tomatoes which are out [ripening on top of] the salt barrel. It is very warm today. I have sweat on my lips and on my eyes.*

> *August 23*
> *Frank harnessed Flora on to the rake yesterday afternoon so that some part of it hit her every time she stepped. The result was she threw Frank off backwards, then rushed up to the tent and smashed the axle on the rake by colliding with one of the wagons that stood there. We can not get an axle unless we send to Chicago for it and we need the rake right away. Pa is going to see if he can borrow one from Mr. Peterson. . . .*

Pa fished a little bird out of the
water barrel this noon. It was
nearly dead but we took care of
it and now it has flown away as
happy as a lark. . . .

Ma and Treadway went over to
Petersons to see if they could get a
rake. They came back without any
but had a nice ride anyway. Mr.
Peterson's rake was a wooden
affair which he made himself
and wasn't much use to us.

They are laying the switch on the North Western Railroad at the new town, Myrtle City [later renamed Athol]. Are one mile west of Peterson's. We can see the train with the ties.

August 24
Pa happened to think that perhaps we could make a wooden axle for the rake. So early this morning he got up and commenced one with an ax and a knife. While he was at work, he looked up and saw that several [train] cars at Myrtle City were aflame. [He shouted and] we all climbed out of bed in a hurry to see them

and saw [another] engine and train coming to the rescue as fast as they could. We could see them very plain. How nice it is to see trains on both railroads!

Pa finally made the axle. Treadway worked all day with it and it shows no signs of breaking down yet. Ma went out to drive the reaper this morning and then after dinner. Allie and Eliza Newell came over this afternoon and Ma left her mowing and came in to see them.

9

A View from the Haystack

When she was not working, Fannie's favorite spot was perched high atop the haystack where she could see in all directions. On August twentieth, a beautiful sun-washed day, she had written:

> *Here I sit on the top of the haystack writing. What a lovely, lovely country this is surely. I look to the west and see, about 3 ³/₄ miles off, the train on the North Western Railroad laying track, which is a very encouraging sight to us. I can see Frank driving the horse rake a short ways off. Pa and Treadway were just here with a load of hay but have gone back. . . .*

Land extends as far as the eye can see—a prairie covered with grass and flowers. I see to the east the top of the tent of our friends, the Newells. I believe I see it but I am not certain. The country of Dakota is certainly beautiful.

From her perch on the haystack, Fannie often saw dark clouds on the horizon. They were not always rain clouds but sometimes clouds of black smoke. She had seen a prairie fire on the nineteenth and knew there was little protection for their tents. Their campsite, supplies, farming equipment, and livestock were completely exposed. That evening in the smoky twilight, she wrote:

I hope that the prairie fires will not harm us. I saw one this afternoon which frightened me, a little.

The fire was a long way off and had not come closer, but prairie fires were always a concern.

A bolt of lightening or a spark from a campfire could start a fire. Strong prairie winds in dry weather would spread it quickly. Fire could destroy everything in its path. Sod houses with thick, damp earth walls gave the best protection. Farmers who lived in wooden shanties or tents often cleared all vegetation from a strip around their houses and hay stacks. A cleared strip, or fire break, could sometimes keep a fire from coming closer. Because there were no fire departments to fight fires, homesteaders kept barrels full of water on hand. If a fire came too close, settlers whipped out the flames with water-soaked gunny sacks, but rain was the best defense. And they had been getting enough of that lately.

August 24

Treadway thought they better get in [another] load of hay . . .
as it looked like rain. They tried to get in with it, but it rained
and blew so hard they couldn't get it all. It rained right through
the tent. Everything on the west side was soaking wet. The
shower didn't last long.

The strong wind also cleansed the air of smoke and dust.
Fannie loved the fresh smell of the prairie grasses after a rain-
fall.

I killed three lizards after the rain. Frank saw one under the bed
and it scared Ma fearfully.

10
The End of the Summer

August 25

*Pa, Frank and I went over to Hall's this morning to get our mail
and to carry [his wife] Ada some sugar. The little boys gave me a
lot of wild grapes.*

*We had another storm in the night. The thunder was fearful—
the wind was, too, but it didn't rain very much. It is just awful
hot today. I had a nice bath and feel better than I did.*

Pa and Treadway just brought us a load of hay. Pa is resting in the shade of the haystack. Frank has been raking since dinner but has finished now. Pa got so warm loading hay that he had to quit. I believe he almost had a sunstroke. It is the hottest day we have had in Dakota. The last part of the afternoon there wasn't a bit of breeze and it was almost unbelievable. We had to build a smudge. The mosquitoes were so thick. Ma and I went out and got smoked. It was nice to watch the fire. Looks like rain again.

August 26
It is nice and cool today but foggy and windy, so that they couldn't hay. . . . The sun has shone this afternoon but has now clouded over. . . . Frank and I [took the wagon] over to the rail-road well for water [for the horses]. The water was low and muddy, and there were two little boys there watering cattle, which didn't make the water any clearer.

It was so dark when they started home that Frank and Fannie could see a comet flash across the star-filled sky. They made wishes and then started lustily singing "In the Evening by the Moonlight."

My brother and I were singing on the way home and [as we neared our tent] our dog didn't know us and commenced to bark. Finally he recognized us and came to meet us.

August 27
It is warm again but there is a cool breeze from the south east which helps considerably. Pa and Treadway got in three loads of hay this morning. The wind blew so [hard] they couldn't get in any more. They have started the second stack. John Appleby and Ezra Spink drove up to our tent today. They were trying to find their folks and got lost.

Fannie was filled with sadness. It was time for her and Frank to return to school in Wisconsin.

Frank has just been packing the trunk. . . . It is our last day at our camp on 119, Range 64, Section 11. I can scarcely believe it is the last, but it is evidently true.

Fannie had penned her farewell to Dakota a week earlier from the top of the haystack. She had written in her diary on August 20:

I have spent such a wonderful summer here. I shall never forget it.

11

Building the Town Up and A-Round

Fannie and Frank returned to school, but Wisconsin no longer felt like home. Fannie later wrote, "Mazo didn't look natural and I felt as if Dakota were the best place after all."

With great determination, Pa and Treadway finished breaking the sod on their quarters. Later in the fall, Pa planted wheat. On the land where they had camped, the men built a small wooden farm house and barn for the horses and farm equipment.

The new town of Mellette now had a depot, and the first official train came to town the next year. William Dale built the first store and set up the town's post office, where he became the postmaster. True W. Child built Mellette's third building, and when printer Andrew Hess came in December, he set up his printing press in Child's store. He called his newspaper the *Western Enterprise* and printed it on brown wrapping paper.

In 1882, Pa had all the family's belongings, farm machinery, animals, and goods from their store and lumberyard in Wisconsin shipped to Mellette. It filled about fifteen train cars. It was reported to be the largest shipment that ever came into Mellette. When Fannie and Frank rejoined the family that summer, Frank and his father formed a partnership, C. M. Howe & Son. They opened a general store and lumberyard

across from the new railroad tracks. Fannie was too busy to write in her diary.

Now new settlers who arrived on the railroad could buy all the supplies they needed at Howe's general store. Tallow candles, kerosene, pickled pork, and tobacco were some of the staples most in demand. Butter and eggs came in big barrels. The eggs came packed in oats. Some farmers were only able to pay their bill in the fall after their first crop had been harvested. Pa and Frank understood and gave them credit in the store. If the new homesteader was lucky with his crops, perhaps in a year or so he could improve his sod house or build one with lumber from their lumberyard.

The spring of 1883 brought even more settlers to the James River Valley—as many as eight carloads a day. They came from Wisconsin, Minnesota, Illinois, and Michigan—lively young people who had come to take up land and make homes. Schools were built and churches started. Mellette now had thirty-nine businesses, as well as doctors, dentists, a lawyer, hotels, and an undertaker. The newspaper changed its name to the *Mellette Tribune*. "The lumber yards of C. M. Howe and Hunter & Cole are scenes of business excitement," the *Tribune* reported in March 1883. "Load after load of lumber is being started off to be made up into pleasant homes."

The early 1880s were good harvest years for the new homesteaders. Bumper crops meant that farmers needed places to store their grain while waiting to sell and ship it back to the eastern mills. These high storage buildings were called elevators. Some farmers got together and formed a co-operative group and elected Pa as president and Frank as treasurer.

One day in 1884, a builder from Minneapolis came through Mellette with a crew of men. He claimed that round elevators were far more resistant to prairie winds than the usual rectangular buildings. That made sense to Pa. He hired the Minneapolis contractor to build the First Farmers Elevator on the railroad siding across the street from their store. From there, the grain could be loaded directly into train cars and shipped out quickly.

To the surprise of the townspeople, a round building took shape on the spot. It was open in the center, from the work floor to the cupola. Bins for the storage of grain surrounded the center space, nesting like segments of an orange against the outer walls. Inside the tall building, a loop of cable with buckets attached hoisted the grain up to the high bins. When the elevator was finished, Pa was so pleased that he asked the builder to build a round house, as well.

Pa had some ideas of his own about how to build his new

house. During his years at sea, he had learned the behavior of the weather—the changing positions of the sun and the effects of the wind. He designed the porch roof so that it reached out just far enough to shade the lower portion of the house when the hot summer sun was high in the sky. Even in the hottest weather, his house would be cool and comfortable. When the sun hung lower in the sky in the winter, rays of sun would shine through the windows and help warm the rooms. Pa also remembered the beautiful houses in the sea ports of New England, grand houses with tall towers from which one could view the wide ocean. Now he would have a house as fine. He told the contractor exactly how to build his round house on the prairie.

All the time the house was being built, Fannie was visiting family in Vermont. She knew Pa was building a house in town, but no one told her what it would be like.

12

A Christmas Surprise

In December 1884, Ma and Pa also went to Vermont, and after a brief visit with their relatives, they rode the train back with Fannie to Dakota. Fannie was delighted to return, to see Frank again, and to be home for Christmas. Even the dog Pete had remembered her and greeted her with happy barks and tail wagging. Right after dinner, Pa and Ma took Fannie over to see the new house, which was almost finished. Fannie gasped in astonishment as she looked up at the tall observation tower, then ran inside to see every room for herself.

She opened the front door and found herself in a round room with a circular staircase carved from solid black walnut. It wound from the entry to the second floor. Looking up, she could see that it circled even higher above. She paused in wonder, then quickly ran into the next rooms.

In the round center of the house were three rooms, like a pie cut into three pieces. The first was a library with walls lined with book shelves, followed by a parlor with a maroon velvet sofa and chair and a three-legged table with a marble top. Even her piano was there. The third room was a bedroom for her parents. Fannie had never seen any house like this before. She marveled at the double folding doors that opened up each room to the next and the ten-foot ceilings. The dining room was a smaller oval room with the kitchen in back of the house.

Opening another door, Fannie discovered the back stairway and, in her eagerness to see the rest of the house, climbed them two at a time. Quickly passing through a storage area,

she opened a door into one of the three upstairs bedrooms. From that, another wide door opened into her bedroom, and she exclaimed in delight as she discovered that there was a small pump organ in the corner.

But there was more to see. Outside her room, the circular stairs wound higher to a third-floor attic, and up, up, higher still to the fourth-floor tower. She scampered up the twisting stairway, till at last she reached the tower and stood breathlessly, turning around and around and around again. This ten-foot-wide round reading room had windows opening to all directions above the roof of the house. Bookcases were built beneath the windows.

The room was high—higher than sitting on the haystack—and she could see so much more: the roof of their store next door, the new houses beyond, the schoolhouse under construction, the grain elevators and depot, and over on Main Street, Postmaster Dale's store, the hotel, and the bank. From this tower, she could also see the train tracks going north to Aberdeen and south to Redfield. And even farther away, Fannie could see new farms and homesteads in the white fields of snow and beyond, to the edge of the earth, where no one could see more because, truly, the earth was round.

That night, Fannie wrote once more in her diary:

December 24, 1884
Pa [has been] building a castle—and they never let me know a word about it!

December 25
Christmas. It is the coldest day of the season. Thermometer at Dale's said 43 below zero. Wind blows a gale from the south. We moved part of our things [from the farmhouse] to the new house and had dinner there. Ma and I are going to sleep there [tonight].

The Round House was a true Christmas surprise, but it was also a lookout tower for all seasons. When summer came, the white blanket of snow would become a sea of golden, waving wheat.

What Happened Next
From Fannie Howe to Me

This story, as told in the words of Fannie Sabra Howe's diary, is true. Fannie was my great aunt, and she recorded her experiences in the summer of 1881 and the winter of 1884. The text of her diary has been passed down in the Howe family ever since. All the people mentioned in this story were real people, and the excerpts from Fannie's diary appear largely as she wrote them.

Fannie Sabra Howe

The words that shape the story around the diary entries are mine. Using family letters and historical accounts, I have filled out the story of how and why things were happening. In a few cases, I used my imagination to move the story along, but I have tried to paint a faithful picture of what Dakota Territory was like in the 1880s.

Fannie's father, who was my great-grand-father Charles Morgan Howe, was always called C. M. His son, the Frank of this book, was my grandfather, Frank Azro Howe, known as F. A. Frank and Fannie attended the University of Wisconsin, graduating together. Fannie majored in music and languages (her diary is sprinkled with brief French passages that have been translated

Charles Morgan Howe

59

Frank Azro Howe

for readers). Frank graduated with honors in chemistry but gave up his dream of graduate studies at Johns Hopkins to go into partnership with his father in Mellette.

C. M. and F. A. Howe started their partnership in 1882. F. A. bought the *Mellette Tribune* in 1886 and became its editor and publisher. He and his father would also build a total of three grain elevators, but the second two were not round. Both men held various positions on the town council and school board. The Howes' Dakota dreams came true, and the family was prosperous and well respected.

Mellette, South Dakota

The Round House, Mellette

60

The Howes' Round House saw great joy and sorrow over the years. Mary Jane Howe, C. M.'s wife and the mother in this story, entered into the social life of the new community with enthusiasm. Under her care, the Howe home became the center of much merriment for the young people of Mellette. Before long, Fannie was courted by Leroy ("Roy") Hedges, a farmer and son

Mary Jane Bickford Howe

of early homesteader W. H. Hedges, the county surveyor. The *Mellette Tribune* records their wedding of June 29, 1885. The wedding party descended the magnificent circular staircase into "the spacious front parlor, where, standing beneath a large bell of wild anemones, they were united in marriage. . . .

Circular staircase, Round House

The congratulations of friends followed, after which the party retired to the dining room and partook of the hospitality of Mrs. Howe's table, which was loaded with many delicacies which she knows so well how to provide. The remainder of the evening was spent in social pleasure, singing and instrumental music."

Sadly, Fannie's life was to be a short one. After they married, Fannie and Roy lived for a few years in Mellette where their two boys, Ernest Howe Hedges and Hiram Clark Hedges, were born. In October 1889, Fannie and her children moved to Chicago to join her husband, who had just started school at the medical college. She caught a severe cold and died ten days later. She was buried in the cemetery in Mellette. Roy and his boys thereafter made their home in Chicago.

Back in what was now the state of South Dakota, C. M. and F. A. Howe closed their general store, but kept their other busi-

Elevator row, Mellette

nesses. Farming in Dakota was always a cycle of boom or bust. The early 1880s had been good years, but in 1889 a terrible drought started. Many settlers left during this Great Dakota Bust. It was hard for farmers to make a living with only one hundred sixty acres and no other income. Many sold their land and moved on to find better opportunities. C. M. Howe & Son were protected by their other businesses during times of bad weather and bad harvests. They bought additional quarters of land from those who left and set up a large farming op-

eration. In time, they moved their headquarters from the original homestead of this story to NW 26. There they had machinery, mules, a cook house on wheels, a house for the superintendent, bunk houses for the crew, and barns (some of straw). When it came time to harvest, the outfit moved out as a unit. The operation was large enough to bind and shock a quarter section—one hundred sixty acres—a day.

In 1892, F. A. Howe married my grandmother, Gertrude Bennett. My father, Charles, and his sisters, Frances and Mary, were born in

Gertrude Bennett Howe Mellette. Soon F. A. bought a winter home in

Charles Morgan Howe with Frank's children, Charles, Frances, and Mary Howe

Long Beach, California, to escape the cold Dakota winters. After Mary Jane Howe died in 1899, C. M. spent the winters with Frank. The family returned to the Round House in Mellette each spring. Once again, times were booming in Dakota, but other changes were also taking place. Motorized farming equipment was replacing large crews and teams of horses. About 1907, C. M. and F. A. divided their operations and sold some land. C. M. died two years later. Frank Howe moved to Minneapolis, where he had a partnership in an automobile business. He still kept his interests in Dakota.

At the end of World War I (1914–1918), farm prices sank again and hard times affected Dakota farmers for the next ten

Views of the Round House

years. Banks failed or called in loans. In 1923, my grandparents moved back to the Round House in Mellette to pay full attention to their farming, oil, and coal businesses. My father, now married, completed his graduate degree and was teaching in a university. He continued the family practice of returning to Dakota for the harvest. The market bust of 1929 and the Great Depression of the 1930s compounded the dire situation of Dakota farmers. It must have been a difficult time in the Round House. After a short illness F. A. died in 1936, leaving what was left of the business in the hands of my father and his sisters, Frances and Mary.

What must have been a chore for my father was sheer delight for me. Every summer, Dad took his vacation time to go to Dakota. This was the Dirty Thirties, when years of drought dried up the fields. Dust storms, grasshopper plagues, and severe winters caused more misery. Farmers could not pay their taxes; stores closed for lack of business. Like all the rest, my father was trying to hold on to the few remaining acres of land

for his family. We were land poor! There was no money to pay taxes or loans, and much land was lost to the banks.

Mellette at that time looked no different from other farming towns. Everything was broken down, dingy, and covered with dust. But I was enchanted with this different world. We stayed in the Round House, which was full of magic, wonder, and terror. At night, I was awakened by the eerie howling of fierce prairie winds that created ghost-like shapes from my curtains. I was frightened by the crashes and booms of heat storms as they rattled the old window panes, and I could hear the mice scurrying about in the attic above me. Ah, . . . but the magic would reappear each dawn.

Fannie's organ was in my bedroom. I pulled and pushed the stops and made wild sounds as I frantically worked the pedals. I explored all the nooks and crannies of the old Round House and discovered hidden treasures. I found old-fashioned paper dolls to cut out, and I studied the clothes in the stacks of ancient ladies' magazines. I imagined myself wearing such exotic fashions. Using old shawls, discarded feathers, and long strings of beads, I pranced about the house and entertained my doll at tea in the parlor. I spent hours looking at 3-D pictures in the stereopticon. I found a collection of old black silk parasols, with carved wooden handles, gold satin linings, and fringe that danced.

But the greatest joy of all was tagging after my father, now dressed in overalls instead of his Washington business suit. I followed him to the family elevator across the street, where I sat at the roll-top desk in the small office and punched numbers on the adding machine. I would race into the elevator each time a dusty truck rumbled in to deliver wheat. Other times, Dad and I bumped along dusty, rutted roads in our old car as he checked if this field or that was ready for harvest. Puppy-dog-like, in the way and underfoot, I did not want to miss a thing! I loved hearing the farmers tell stories of C. M. and my grandparents in the early days. Who needed Caddie Woodlawn and Laura Ingalls Wilder! This was *my* family house on the prairie.

During World War II (1939–1945), new markets for grain and good weather again brought top prices for crops. Even so, the demands of his job in Washington made it impossible for my father to spend so much time on the family business. In 1945, the remaining land was divided among the three children of Frank A. Howe, and the belongings of seventy years and two generations were cleared out of the Round House so that it could be rented. Fannie's diary was found amid the piles of papers. Copies of this precious record were typed and given to family members. The original diary was sent to Fannie's granddaughter, Myra Hedges, in Chicago, but contact with Fannie's family was lost after that. It would be wonderful if surviving relatives and the actual diary could be located again.

Cleaning out the Round House proved to be a herculean task. Many of great-grandfather's books went to the Mellette library. Some of the remaining furniture was sent to a museum in Watertown. Hundreds of items and pounds of papers and records, plus the contents of the old general store, were sent to the South Dakota State Historical Society in Pierre. Some of those items can still be seen today at the society's headquarters in the South Dakota Cultural Heritage Center. The friend-

Mary Jane Howe's remembrance quilt

ship quilt that accompanied the family to Dakota from Wisconsin came to me. Today it, too, is in the Cultural Heritage Center.

By 1950, the Round House was old and needed renovation, which nobody could afford. The house and remaining elevator were sold in 1958 to the South Dakota Wheat Growers Association. In the end, the building proved too expensive to keep up and was sold to a salvage company. Without my father's knowledge, it was demolished in 1964. My father said he would have given the house away if it could have been conserved. It was reported that some out-of-state hunters bought the spectacular walnut circular staircase and took it to Kentucky.

This is almost the end of the story. The Round House and the carriage house, the old store, and the Howe elevators have all vanished along with three generations of Howes. Only

The Round House in disrepair

some land remains, thanks to three generations of hard-working farmers, the Robertsons, the Arthurs, and the Francolis. They still help us farm some of C. M.'s land and keep the dreams alive. In 1983, when I was visiting Violet Robertson, she gave me a ceramic plaque of the logo prepared for the 1981 Mellette centennial celebration. The drawing depicted the homesteader farmer, the train depot, and the Round House tower. Her kindness rekindled many old memories. That plaque still hangs on my wall next to an old photograph of the round house and elevator. Now Fannie's diary makes the story live again.

SOURCES

The American Heritage Cookbook and Illustrated History of American Eating & Drinking. New York: American Heritage Publishing Co., 1964.

Beebe, Lucius, and Charles Clegg. *The American West: The Pictorial Epic of a Continent*. New York: Random House, 1989.

Brooks, Allyson, and Steph Jacon. *Homesteading and Agricultural Development Context*. Vermillion: South Dakota State Historical Preservation Center, 1994.

Bruno, Leonard C. *Science & Technology Firsts*. Detroit, Mich.: Gale Research, 1997.

Bunkers, Suzanne L., ed., with Ann Hodgson. *A Pioneer Farm Girl: The Diary of Sarah Gillespie, 1877-1878*. Mankato, Minn.: Blue Earth Books, 2000.

Crellin, John K., and Jane Philpot. *Herbal Medicine, Past and Present*. Vol. 2: *A Reference Guide to Medicinal Plants*. Durham, N.C.: Duke University Press, 1990.

Davidson, Alan. *Oxford Companion to Food*. Oxford, U.K.: Oxford University Press, 1999.

Derry, T. K., and Trevor I. Williams. *A Short History of Technology from the Earliest Times to A.D. 1900*. New York: Oxford University Press, 1961.

Gutcheon, Beth. *The Perfect Patchwork Primer*. New York: David McKay Co., 1973.

Hague, Frank O. *Memories of Bygone Days in Dakota Territory*. Bath, N.Y.: Iras K. Hague & Amburn R. Hague, 1966.

Harlow, Dana D. *Prairie Echoes: Spink County in the Making*. Aberdeen, S.Dak.: By the Author, 1961.

Hibbard, Benjamin H. *A History of the Public Land Policies*. Madison: University of Wisconsin Press, 1965.

Holt, O. H. *Dakota: "Behold, I show you a delightsome land."* Chicago: Rand, McNally & Co., 1885.

Howe Family Papers. Private Collection.

Johnson, James R., and Gary E. Larson. *Grassland Plants of South Dakota and the Northern Great Plains*. Brookings: South Dakota State University, 1999.

Mellette Tribune, 29 Mar. 1883, 2 July 1885.

Moulton, Candy. *The Writer's Guide to Everyday Life in the Wild West*. Cincinnati, Ohio: Writer's Digest Books, 1999.

Nolan, Leta Anne, proj. dir. *History of the Spink County Area: In Celebration of South Dakota's Centennial, 1889-1989*. Dallas, Tex.: Curtis Media Corp., 1989.

Olkowski, William, Sheila Daar, and Helga Olkowski. *Common-Sense Pest Control*. Newtown, Conn.: Taunton Press, 1991.

Over, William H. *Wild Flowers of South Dakota*. Vermillion: University of South Dakota, 1942.

Reese, John B. *Some Pioneers and Pilgrims on the Prairies of Dakota*; or, *From the Ox Team to the Aeroplane*. Mitchell, S.Dak.: By the Author, 1920.

Taber, Clarence W. *Breaking Sod on the Prairies: A Story of Early Days in Dakota*. Yonkers-on-Hudson, N.Y.: World Book Co., 1924.

Towne, Arthur E. *Old Prairie Days: A Historic Narrative of the Stirring Pioneer Days in Dakota Territory in the Eighties*. Otsego, Mich.: Otsego Union Press, 1941.

WORDS TO KNOW

arid—lacking water, very dry

buffalo chips—chunks of dried manure left on the prairie by herds of buffalo; burned for heat in stoves or outdoor fires

bumper crop—a harvest of wheat or other crop that is larger than usual

calico—cotton material with a colorful all-over print or design, often of small flowers

casing—a metal or wooden tube used to line the wall of a water well

circumference—the distance around a circle

cordial—warm and sincere in manner

crimping pins—an early type of hair curler used to form small, tight waves or curls

cupola—a small dome built on top of the roof of a building

dysentery—any variety of stomach problems with pain and diarrhea; often caused by contaminated food or water

gunny sack—a bag made of rough burlap cloth

herculean—something hard to do; needing the strength of the mythical character Hercules

melodeon—a small musical organ or piano-like instrument. When the player pushed on the foot pedals, bellows sucked air through reeds to create the music played on the keys.

shanty—a small, roughly built cabin or hut

smudge—a smoky fire built in a heavy iron pot

squatted—occupied land without filing for it in order to gain title to it *staples*—food items used most often in a household

stereopticon—a picture viewer that allowed people to see photographs in three dimensions, or 3-D

ulster—a long, narrow, belted overcoat that protected
clothing for travelers

INDEX

ACKNOWLEDGEMENTS

My cousins, Dr. Clif Hamilton, Martha Hamilton Dickey, and Marn Hamilton, graciously and readily agreed to the publication of Fannie Howe's diary. Marn was particularly encouraging and gave me access to the old Howe family pictures and papers. Thank you to the Library of Congress and its helpful staff, especially Dr. Sybille Jagusch of the Children's Literature Center. Cliff Oberle at the Mellette Bank generously shared his collection of old Mellette pictures. He is descended from one of the earliest settlers. Thanks also to Marty Francoli who introduced me to his delightful grandmother, Frances Spink Braun, who straightened out for me the family relationships of the Spinks, Applebys, and Newells. Frances's grandfather, Ezra, was the brother of Hall in this story. Her father, Percy, lived at the Howe farm when Frances was a little girl. A special thank you to Nancy Tystad Koupal, my editor and publisher, who with her guidance and suggestions, to my surprise and delight, turned my story into a book. As chauffeur par excellence, my husband drove miles around the Midwest so that I could see a sod hut, old farm machinery, and visit prairie museums. Thanks, Ed, for all your patience and help.

PICTURE CREDITS

Most of the photographs in "What Happened Next" are from members of the Howe family, except those of Fannie S. and Frank Howe, which are their graduation photographs, courtesy of the University of Wisconsin–Madison Archives. The quilt photograph is by Chad Coppess, South Dakota Department of Tourism and State Development.